The Boy Who Learned

Upside Down

Based on a True Story

Christy Scattarella

Illustrated by Winky Wheeler

*Promise me you'll always remember:
You're braver than you believe,
and stronger than you seem,
and smarter than you think.*

~A.A. Milne

To Ken, Alex

and of course, Shadow

~ Christy

To my family:

Kiki, Woody, Cricket,

Pat, Kelly and Ryan

and my love, J'aime

I love you all!

~ Winky

N ot again!

Alex stared at his book report. Red marks covered it like chickenpox. *What's wrong with me?* he thought. *I never get anything right.*

"Look what I got!" squealed Sabrina.

Her paper was perfect. Even her handwriting was perfect. Alex crumpled his report and stuffed it in his backpack, where nobody could see it.

"It's time for silent reading," said Mrs. Foster. "Let's take out our books."

Let's not, thought Alex. But he opened his book anyway. As he ran his finger under each line, the letters began to wiggle and squirm. "Hold still!" he hissed, pressing his finger down to stop them.

It was no use! "S" slithered away like a snake. "C" turned a cartwheel so it looked like a "U". "P" popped right off the page. Suddenly whole words seemed to be jumping out of the book and scurrying down the hall. Alex slumped in his seat. Reading was too hard. Everything about school was too hard.

I give up, thought Alex.

He closed his eyes and thought about his dog Shadow instead. She didn't care about reading or grades. Whenever she saw him, she licked his face and wagged her whole body along with her tail.

He imagined Shadow at his side, ready to rescue him from reading.

"Fetch!" he'd command, and she'd bound down the hall, hot on the scent of runaway words. She'd plop them back in the book, still slimy from her jaws. The letters would lie there, too worn out to wiggle, and Alex could finally read them.

"Alex!" Mrs. Foster interrupted his daydream. "Don't forget. It's your first day with Mrs. Sandy."

Alex's heart sank. Mrs. Sandy's room was the place for kids who had trouble learning.

"You can go with Mary," said Mrs. Foster. "She'll show you the way." Mary was new this year. Each morning she had to walk out in front of the whole class while everyone watched. Alex always felt sorry for her. But now thirty-two pairs of eyes were following him as he walked across the room. His sneakers squeaked like trapped mice.

"Where's he going?" asked Sabrina.

"Special class," said Nathan. Alex wanted to disappear.

Why did he have to be "special"?

Why couldn't he just be like everyone else?

Alex let Mary go ahead. He dragged his feet down the hall like he was heading off to a dungeon. He imagined a dark pit where gigantic books were stacked to the top, blocking out the light. Books with tiny letters and no pictures, letters leaping like frogs in every direction. Alex felt doomed.

With a shaking hand, he reached for the door.

But when he stepped into the classroom, he couldn't believe his eyes. Sunlight streamed into the room. A tower of stuffed animals stretched to the ceiling. Striped tigers, fluffy dogs, and grinning monkeys peeked out from the pile.

At the tip-top perched the most outrageous animal of all.

A RAT!

But not just any old rat. This rat had glow-in-the-dark eyes, gnarly fangs and sticky suction-cup paws. Its fur was the color of a chocolate milkshake. Alex stared at the rat. Beady eyeballs stared right back. "Whoa!" said Alex. "What a rat!"

Then he heard a voice say, "How would you like to earn that rat?"

Alex turned to see Mrs. Sandy. "Really?" he asked. "To keep? How?"

"You can earn it by being a courageous student," said Mrs. Sandy.

A courageous student? Alex gulped. Him? Brave? Courage was for knights, or superheroes, not for someone like him. But he wanted the rat. He took a deep breath and asked, "What do I have to do?"

"Three things," said Mrs. Sandy. "First, tell yourself *I can!* instead of *I can't.* It takes courage not to give up when something is hard—and that includes school. Next, help someone else. That takes courage, too. And finally, believe in yourself. That takes the most courage of all. Think you're up for it?"

Alex wasn't sure he could do any of those things. What did that even mean, *believe in yourself*? But he looked at Mrs. Sandy and nodded. For that beady-eyed rat he was willing to try.

Alex had never worked so hard in his whole life. He was doing his best. Every day in class, he stayed in his seat even when it felt like ants from the class ant farm were running up and down his legs.

At night, he turned off the TV and did his reading homework. The letters still wiggled and squirmed, but under Shadow's watchful gaze, only the sneakiest letters crept off the page.

I can do this, Alex told himself.

I can!

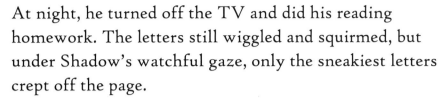

One morning before school, Alex saw Mary running across the playground, her backpack overflowing as usual. *Whoosh!* She slipped on a patch of slimy leaves. *Thud!* She hit the ground. Papers shot out of her backpack and fluttered to the ground like dying leaves. One sheet landed right at Sabrina's feet.

"Look!" Sabrina hooted, pointing to the messy block letters. "Baby handwriting!"

A hush fell over the schoolyard. A swing squeaked in the breeze. As Mary began picking up her homework, Alex saw tears in her eyes. He wanted to help her, but then the other kids would make fun of him, too!

Then he remembered: *It takes courage to help someone else.* Alex took a deep breath and stepped right up to Sabrina. "Mary's just as good as you are," he said. "So leave her alone." Sabrina opened her mouth and closed it again.

Just then the bell rang. "Thanks," said Mary, as everyone ran inside.

Alex just shrugged. But as he kneeled down to help gather her papers, he thought, *Wow! Did I really do that?*

Alex couldn't stop staring at the world's most outrageous rat. *Tomorrow you're coming home with me!* Alex was sure the rat winked at him.

Then Mrs. Sandy said, "Class, don't forget, before we choose stuffed animals tomorrow, we're going to have a spelling test."

Oh, NO! Alex had forgotten. Spelling made Alex feel stupid. Too many letters looked one way and and sounded another, and sometimes they didn't make any sound at all! Alex imagined silent "L's" and "E's" creeping around on tiptoe, trying to trip him up. *I'd rather pour milk on a bowl of broccoli and eat it for breakfast,* Alex thought. He gazed once more at the rat. This time, those glassy eyeballs stared right past him.

At lunch, Alex couldn't swallow more than one bite of his peanut butter and jelly sandwich. He shoved the rest into his pack. A lump of dread rose in his throat and stuck there.

Alex avoided his spelling all afternoon. By evening, he could stall no longer. But the spelling list wasn't on his desk, or in his closet, or under his bed. Alex tore the room apart, but the list had vanished.

"Why do I lose everything?" he moaned. "What's wrong with me, Shadow?" But Shadow wasn't listening. Her head was in his backpack.

"It's like I'm upside down. Things go in my brain, then fall right back out. Why can't I just be like everyone else?"

Shadow snorted. Then she shook her head. The pack flew off. Out tumbled a pile of crumpled papers, and one of them . . .

"My spelling list!" cried Alex in relief. But then he gasped. The list was smeared with peanut butter and jelly from his leftover lunch. Forget spelling the words—now he couldn't even read them!

"I give up," said Alex. He couldn't face school tomorrow, maybe not ever again. He closed his eyes and imagined himself and Shadow on a desert island where homework was against the law and spelling bees were just bees that knew how to spell.

Meanwhile, Shadow gave the list another lick. She licked and slurped until Alex finally opened his eyes. "Hey, stop that!" he said. Then he stared. Shadow had licked the list clean!

Now she licked Alex's face and her whole body wagged along with her tail.

That night, Alex and Shadow studied spelling words until bedtime. They missed their favorite TV show and never even noticed.

"*H*ome," said Mrs. Sandy. "I live at home." Alex gripped his pencil and wrote H-O-M-E. The first word on the spelling test and he knew he got it right.

"The next word is *comb*," said Mrs. Sandy. Alex scribbled down the answer, then looked around. No one else was writing. That was one of those tricky words. It had stopped the spellers cold in their tracks. Mary looked ready to snap her pencil in half.

"Mrs. Sandy?" blurted Alex. "I made up a clue for comb. Can I share it with the class?"

"Alex, this is a test."

"But shouldn't we help other people?"

Mrs. Sandy tilted her head to one side. She nodded and smiled.

Alex looked at the class. "In my head, I see pictures, and for this word, I saw a boy using a comb. 'B' is for boy. So *comb* ends with a . . . "

The other kids started writing. His clue had worked!

Mrs. Sandy corrected the tests and handed them back. Alex didn't get all the words right, but for the first time ever he got more right than wrong.

"Great job, class," said Mrs. Sandy. "And now it's time!" One by one, every kid chose a stuffed animal. Mary picked out a giant black cat and hugged it close.

"We didn't have anything like this at my old school," she whispered to Alex. He'd never seen such a big smile on her face.

Then it was his turn.

"Congratulations, Alex," said Mrs Sandy. "You're a courageous student. You didn't give up. You helped others. And I think you believe in yourself more, too."

Alex still wasn't sure what that last part meant, but he didn't care.

He had the rat.

At lunch, Alex peeked in his backpack. Creepy eyeballs glowed back at him. His mom had packed his favorite lunch, a cheddar cheese and pickle sandwich, but Alex was too excited to eat more than one bite. He shoved the rest of the sandwich back in his pack.

When he got home, he'd stick the rat's suction feet on the living-room mirror. Or maybe on the window, where everyone could see. He imagined his class stopping by. No, make that the whole school—a school-wide field trip to admire Alex's rat! He could almost hear children cheering, and News Chopper 2 swooping down for a look, and bells ringing. Bells?

The tardy bell!

Alex snapped out of his daydream and raced off to class.

"Yikes!" Alex's mom yelped when she saw a beady-eyed rodent in her living room.

"It's the most amazing rat ever," said Alex. "And I earned it!"

Mom smiled. "That's wonderful, Alex. I'm really proud of you. But you're going to have to take it down."

"Why? I like it there."

Mom shook her head firmly. "Your rat doesn't belong there. Toys belong in your room. Besides, this one smells funny. If I didn't know better, I'd say your rat has been eating cheese and pickles."

Alex sighed and loosened the suction cups. With Shadow at his heels, Alex carried the rat to his room. He'd find the perfect spot for it later.

That evening, Alex wolfed
down his dinner. He couldn't
wait to see his rat's eerie
eyeballs glowing in the dark.
But when he opened his
bedroom door, he let out a cry.

Next to his bed sat Shadow. Tufts of fluff were stuck to her mouth. A suction cup paw lay by her side.

"Shaaadooo-ooww!" cried Alex in horror. "How could you?!"

Shadow's head dropped. Her ears drooped. Her big brown eyes gazed up at him.

"Oh Shadow," whispered Alex, his voice trembling.

"This isn't like you. You never get into my stuff . . . unless
I've got food." Alex held the rat up to his nose and took
a big whiff. Yow! Cheese and pickles! Now it all made
terrible sense. *My lunch! Shadow ate my leftover sandwich
and thought my rat was dessert!*

"I'm sorry, Shadow. I know you didn't mean to hurt my
rat," he whispered. "You helped me earn it. You wouldn't
let me give up. I just wish you didn't like cheese and pickles
so much."

Alex's mom poked her head in the door and saw the
disaster. "Oh, honey! Your poor rat. Don't worry," she said.
"I'll get you another one."

"Mom, you can NEVER get me another one," wailed Alex,
choking back his tears. "This rat was special because I
EARNED IT."

Later, Alex's mom called him into the living room. On the coffee table lay a needle, thread, and a rat that needed surgery. "Think we can fix him?" she asked.

Alex thought for a moment. "I know we can."

An hour later, the operation was complete.

Stiches laced up the rat's belly, and one ear was
crooked, but Alex didn't mind. The rat reminded
him of his courageous journey. Alex thought about
all that he had accomplished. He didn't give up.
He tackled sneaky spelling words and helped his
friends, too.

I did all that, he told himself, *not by being like
everyone else, but by being ME.*

At that moment, Alex got an idea. A big, bold,
super-duper different idea.

He darted down the hall to his room and returned with his arms full of stuffed animals. "These are for Mary's old school," he told his mom, "to help kids like me believe in themselves.

"They can even have their own special day," he said. "And I know just what to call it!"

That's how Mary's school had the very first Shadow Day. Boys and girls celebrated their courage and kindness, and turning *I can't* into *I can!*

Soon other schools started their own Shadow Days. Teachers posted Shadow's picture in their classrooms to remind students to believe in themselves, because that takes the most courage of all.

Over the years, thousands of children celebrated Shadow Day. Sometimes, Alex and Shadow visited their classrooms. "Reading and writing are still hard for me, but I don't give up," Alex would say.

"I have what it takes. And so do you!"

Sometimes, School Takes Courage

This story is based on a real boy named Alex who turned *"I can't" into "I can!"* and Shadow, the dog who loved him. School was hard for Alex. He has learning challenges that turn reading into an endless chase after runaway words and make it difficult to pay attention, focus and follow directions — as if he's learning upside down.

Photo Credit: Kraig Scattarella

For youngsters like Alex the struggle to read, to write, and to belong often becomes too much. They decide: *I can't.* And they give up, on school and on themselves. But with understanding and support, kids with learning differences can grow up to *make* a difference. Artists, athletes and entrepreneurs who once wondered, "What's wrong with me?" have gone on to change the world.

Inspired by his real-life journey Alex and his mom created The Shadow Project — named after you-know-who — to provide tools and support for kids who learn differently. Starting with Mrs. 'Sandy' Cechinni in Portland, Oregon, The Shadow Project has teamed up with special education teachers to help more than 6,500 boys and girls discover they are courageous and capable learners. And that reminds all of us to celebrate the differences that make us unique.

Alex is grown now and continues to help The Shadow Project. To this day he still uses clues to spell hard words like comb.

Photo Credit: Ken Moore

The author's proceeds from the sale of this book benefit children with learning challenges through The Shadow Project.

Photo Credit: Kraig Scattarella

Visit shadow-project.org

Christy Scattarella started The Shadow Project, named after her son Alex's mischievous mutt, Shadow, as a tiny operation in a special education classroom. Since its launch, The Shadow Project has teamed with teachers to help more than 6,500 boys and girls recognize themselves as capable, courageous, and able to learn. Christy is the nonprofit's executive director. She has been honored locally and nationally for helping children with learning disabilities to discover their potential. She is the recipient of Portland, Oregon's Making a Difference in Education Award, was named Education Citizen of the Year by the Oregon Education Association, and was chosen as one of Nabisco's 100 Extraordinary Women. She was a reporter at The Seattle Times and Willamette Week, and has worked on documentaries for the History Channel. She lives in Portland, Oregon.

Winky Wheeler began drawing before she was two. In the sixth grade the children were asked what they thought they would be in the year 2000. Winky's first thought was that she would be very, very old. But she also knew she would be an artist. Today her whimsical, vivid watercolors are internationally distributed on fabric design, puzzles, flags, ornaments, posters, and greeting cards. A graduate of the School of Visual Arts and a native New Yorker, she now lives in Portland, Oregon.